Everyday English for
HOSPITALITY PROFESSIONALS

Lawrence J. Zwier
Michigan State University

with

Nigel Caplan
Michigan State University

Compass
Publishing

Distributed By:
Grass Roots Press
Toll Free: 1-888-303-3213
Fax: (780) 413-6582
Web Site: www.grassrootsbooks.net

Everyday English for
HOSPITALITY PROFESSIONALS

Lawrence J. Zwier with Nigel Caplan

Publisher: Casey Malarcher
Development Editor: Kelly Roubo
Illustrations: Hieram Wientraub
Cover/Interior Design: Dammora Inc.

http://www.compasspub.com
email: info@compasspub.com

ISBN 978-1-59966-075-2

20 19 18 17 16 15 14 13 12 11

To the Teacher

Everyday English for Hospitality Professionals (EEHP) presents the vocabulary needed for speaking about hospitality work in English. It focuses on 61 activities common in international-class hotels worldwide.

This book may be used in conjunction with the Hospitality English courseware by DynEd International. Further information about this companion product can be found at www.dyned.com. Many of the characters in *EEHP* also appear in Hospitality English, and many vital concepts are covered in both titles—from different perspectives and with different emphases. Hospitality English is especially good for working with spoken English. The emphasis in *EEHP* is on broadening vocabulary through pictures. Together, these two sources offer a well-rounded introduction to the English that hospitality professionals need.

EEHP focuses on verbs. Many other picture-based English books (such as picture dictionaries) have a lot of nouns but not many verbs, adjectives, or other parts of speech. Since a verb is the heart of any sentence, noun-heavy resources often fail to develop much communicative ability in their users.

Most chapters focus on what a hospitality worker does. Some chapters—labeled "The Guest's Experience"—feature a guest's actions instead. These are included because it is important for hospitality workers to learn vocabulary related to certain guest-centered processes.

| Aims |

A few of the aims central to *EEHP* are:
- to activate readers' "event schemata," their sets of expectations about how ordinary hospitality events usually proceed
- to concentrate on the most essential and most picturable steps in those activities
- to create pictorial associations that aid in the storage and retrieval of vocabulary knowledge

EEHP does not intend to teach people how to do hospitality jobs. This can be done very well by the expert personnel at career schools or in company training programs. Our target is language.

| Organization |

Each chapter in *EEHP* is about a process. The chapters are grouped into seven larger sections. The chapters can be studied in any sequence that makes sense for the needs of students. It is not necessary, for example, to do Chapter 14 before Chapter 15. Each one is a self-sufficient lesson on its own. This gives various programs flexibility to focus on what their students need most.

Each chapter has a list of "key vocabulary"—the most important words and phrases from the chapter. The meaning of the key vocabulary items can be found by looking at the pictures that illustrate them. Most chapters also have "Culture and Language" sections to explain vocabulary that is especially challenging.

| Using *EEHP* |

This book can be used as a classroom text or a self-study tool at home. Its language level is high-beginning to low-intermediate, but it can be useful to students at higher levels as well.

We hope your students will enjoy enriching their English vocabularies as they set out for satisfying careers in the hospitality field.

Characters

Bell Service

Don

Concierge

Paul

Driver/ Parking Valet

Teri

Event Planner

Beatriz Chan

Front Desk Clerks

Alberto, Rob, Pat

Front Desk Manager

Maria

Housekeeper

Susan

Restaurant Waitress

Katie

Restaurant Hostess

Emma

Room Service

Cody

Guests

Sam Monroe

Sandra Randall

Nancy Parin

Mr. & Mrs. Porter

Maryn Karini & Family

Jeff Reynolds & Family
(wife Dana, son Brian)

Tom Smith & Family

Others

Mr. Johnson
(calls for reservation)

Mr. Boor
(calls to leave a message)

Mr. Gordon
(makes restaurant
reservation by phone)

Ms. Lopez
(seated in restaurant
without reservation)

Table of **Contents**

Unit V Concierge Services >>

Unit VI Dealing with Problems >>

Unit VII Checking Out >>

Appendix >>

1. Taking a Reservation by Phone

Maryn Karini called the Pine Ridge Hotel to make a reservation.

Pat asked for the dates of her stay.

She pulled up the hotel's reservations calendar on her computer terminal.

Pat asked how many people would be in Maryn's party.

Maryn asked for a double-queen room.

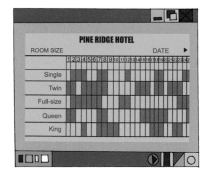

Pat searched the reservation system for availability.

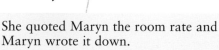

She quoted Maryn the room rate and Maryn wrote it down.

Types of rooms and beds

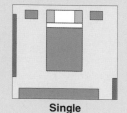
Single

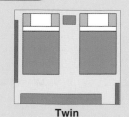
Twin

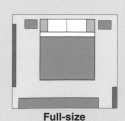
Full-size

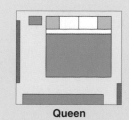
Queen

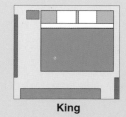
King

Pat asked her to spell her last name and entered her details in the guest database.

The number is 1-2-3-4...

Maryn gave her credit card number to hold the reservation.

When does that expire?

Pat asked for the card's expiration date.

That's one double-queen room for 4 nights...

Pat repeated the details of the booking...

Your confirmation number is....

HT348

...and read Maryn a confirmation number to write down.

Will there be anything else, Mrs. Karini?

Pat checked that the guest was satisfied with the reservation...

See you on the 4th!

...and said goodbye.

Credit Cards

card number

valid from date

expiration date

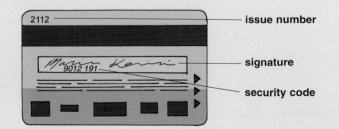

issue number

signature

security code

9

2. Revising a Reservation

Pat answered the phone.

Maryn asked if she could add a night to her reservation.

Pat looked up Maryn's record in the database.

Maryn's room was already allocated to another guest.

Pat offered to upgrade Maryn to a room with a sea view.

Maryn agreed and Pat revised the reservation...

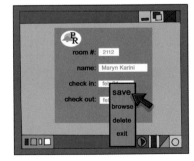

...then she saved the changes.

Culture and Language

- allocate = give out, assign
- *Revise* means "change [something] to make it better"

- When Pat upgrades Maryn's room, she gives Maryn a higher-quality room for the same price as the room she requested.

3. Suggesting Alternative Accommodation

KEY
KEY VOCABULARY

Verbs

call
explain
host
offer
put [put]
suggest

Nouns

accommodation
conference
phone number
reservation
room
vacancy
waiting list

Adjectives

alternative
available
booked

Mr. Johnson called the Pine Ridge Hotel to make a reservation.

However, the hotel was fully booked...

Pat explained that there were no rooms available...

...because the hotel was hosting a large conference.

Pat offered to put him on the waiting list for a room.

She offered to find another hotel with a vacancy.

Pat suggested that the Hilltop Inn might have some rooms.

She gave Mr. Johnson the Hilltop's phone number.

Culture and Language

- As used in this chapter, *booked* means "reserved."

- A *conference* is a very large meeting that draws hundreds of people.

4. The Guest's Experience: Meeting a Hotel Representative at the Airport

KEY VOCABULARY

Verbs

arrive
buckle
climb into
escort
exit
introduce
load
meet [met]
notice
offer
open
radio
slide [slid]
take
thank
welcome

Nouns

area
back
baggage carousel
baggage claim
bag
bench seat
driver's seat
fact
hotel
luggage cart
passenger compartment
passenger door
pleasure
representative
seat belt
shuttle
sign
tip
van

Others

a few (adj.)
meanwhile (adv.)
on the way (adv., prep.)

When Mr. and Mrs. Porter exited the baggage claim area,...

...they noticed Teri holding a sign with their name on it.

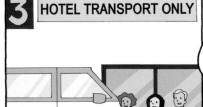

They introduced themselves.

Teri welcomed them to the city.

She offered to take their bags.

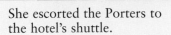

She escorted the Porters to the hotel's shuttle.

She opened the passenger door for them...

...and they climbed into the passenger compartment.

Culture and Language

- Because a shuttle van requires you to step up, you climb into the seat or into the van. Other ways of saying it: *get into your seat, sit down in* your seat.
- *Bags, baggage,* and *luggage* are all used to mean "the set of things a traveler carries." Each individual item is a bag, a *piece of luggage*, or (if large and with a handle) a *suitcase*.

- When Teri speaks into the radio, she uses special words. *Over* means "I'm finished speaking." *Copy that* means "I received your message."
- A normal tip for an airport van driver is about US$2. If the trip is especially long or if the service is especially good, a higher tip might be given.

4. The Guest's Experience: Meeting a Hotel Representative at the Airport

They slid into one of the bench seats and buckled their seat belts.

Meanwhile, Teri loaded their bags into the back of the van.

Teri climbed into the driver's seat...

...and radioed the hotel that she was on the way.

On the way to the hotel, she told the Porters a few facts about the town.

When they arrived at the hotel,...

...the Porters thanked her and gave her a tip.

5. The Guest's Experience: Arriving at the Hotel

KEY VOCABULARY

Verbs

arrive
carry
drop off
follow
give [gave] a tip
lead [led]
ring [rang]
take [took]
tip

Nouns

bellhop
bell
driver
front desk
lobby
revolving door
service
shuttle
tip

Others

in front of (prep.)
thank you (reduced
clause)

The shuttle dropped Sam Monroe off in front of the hotel.

Mr. Monroe tipped the driver.

Don, the bellhop, took Mr. Monroe's bags.

Sam followed Don through the revolving door...

...and into the lobby.

Don led Sam to the front desk.

He rang the bell for service...

...and Sam gave him a tip.

Culture and Language

- A bellhop, also called a bellman or doorman, is often the first person to greet guests as they arrive at a hotel. The bellhop usually helps them with their bags and may escort them to their rooms.

6. Welcoming a Guest 1: With a Reservation

KEY VOCABULARY

Verbs

check in
come [came]
confirm
enter
greet
identify oneself
log in

Nouns

confirmation number
information
password
personnel
reservation
staff room
system
user name

Adjectives

authorized
correct
non-smoking

AUTHORIZED PERSONNEL ONLY

Welcome to the Pine Ridge Hotel.

Alberto came out from the staff room...

...and greeted the guest.

I'd like to check in, please. I have a reservation.

Sam Monroe asked to check in.

My name's Monroe. Sam Monroe.

Sam identified himself.

USERNAME: robster
PASSWORD: ✶✶✶✶✶✶

Alberto logged in to his computer with his user name and password.

Could I have your confirmation number, Mr. Monroe?

He entered Sam's confirmation number.

I have you down for 3 nights. Is that right?

Yes.

He checked that the information in the system was correct.

And that's a non-smoking room.

He confirmed that Mr. Monroe had a non-smoking room.

Culture and Language

- *Information* is a non-count noun.
- You are not permitted to smoke in a *non-smoking* room.
- *confirm* something = make sure about it

- If you *identify yourself*, you tell someone who you are.
- To *enter* information into a computer is to type it so the computer can store it.

7. Welcoming a Guest 2: Without a Reservation

Verbs

apologize
choose [chose]
create
search
suggest
take [took]
wait in line
keep [kept]

Nouns

delay
front desk
night
possibility
record
room log
vacancy

Adjectives

available
new

Sandra Randall waited in line at the front desk.

Pat apologized for the delay.

Sandra asked about a room for the night.

Pat searched the hotel's room log for an available room.

Pat suggested two possibilities.

Sandra chose the king room.

Pat created a new record for Sandra on the computer.

Culture and Language

- *possibilities* = several choices. If you don't want one, you can choose another.

- *wait in line* = stand behind other people until you get your turn to be served

8. Securing the Stay with a Credit Card

Verbs

accept
ask
charge
check out
confirm
explain
nood
secure
sign
swipe
take [took]

Nouns

card reader
clerk
credit card
digit
guest
imprint
record
security

Adjectives

correct
necessary

Rob asked Sam to confirm the last four digits of the credit card in his record.

Sandra asked whether the hotel accepted American Express.

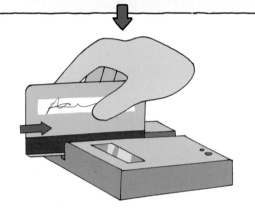

Rob swiped Sam's credit card through the card reader.

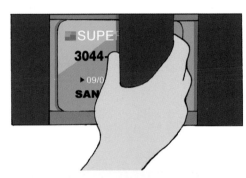

Pat took an imprint of Sandra's credit card as security.

Both clerks explained to their guests that their credit cards would be charged when they checked out.

Culture and Language

- VISA, MasterCard, and American Express are all major credit cards.
- *As security* means "as a way to make sure the hotel is paid for any services the guest uses."

- "Sam's card was swiped" means that his card was passed through a slot in an electronic reader. Sandra's card was used to make an *imprint*, a paper copy made by pressing carbon paper against the raised numbers and letters on the card.

9. Filling out a Registration Form

KEY VOCABULARY

Verbs

correct
fill in
fill out
print out
sign
write [wrote]

Nouns

address
blank
car
city
date of birth
details
error
family name
field
first name
form
license plate
number
registration form
signature
software
state
ZIP

Others

automatically (adv.)

Alberto printed out Mr. Monroe's details on a registration form.

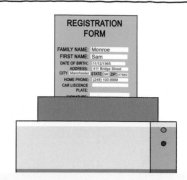

The software automatically filled in some of the fields.

Sam corrected an error on the form.

Sam did not have a car, so he wrote "N/A" in the blank for a license-plate number.

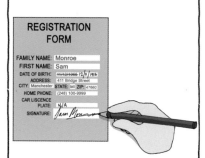

Sam signed the form.

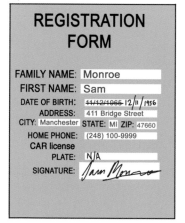

REGISTRATION FORM

FAMILY NAME: Monroe
FIRST NAME: Sam
DATE OF BIRTH: ~~11/12/1965~~ 12/11/1956
ADDRESS: 411 Bridge Street
CITY: Manchester STATE: MI ZIP: 47660
HOME PHONE: (248) 100-9999
CAR license
PLATE: N/A
SIGNATURE: *Sam Monroe*

Culture and Language

- You *fill out* a document with many blank spaces. You *fill in* an individual blank.
- *N/A* = not applicable
- On a form, *ZIP* means "zip code." This is a number indicating a certain postal area. In other countries, it is known as a "postal code."

- *automatically* = by machine, without any effort from a person
- In North America, telephone numbers are often written as, for example, (555) 376-3763. The first three digits, in parentheses, are the area code. The rest of the numbers are for the individual phone line. Sometimes, the parentheses are left out. Then the number is written as 555-376-3763.

10. Escorting a Guest to a Room

KEY VOCABULARY

Verbs

board
get [got] off
escort
insert
lead [led] the way
open
point out
press
pull
put [put]
reach
wheel

Nouns

door
elevator
end
exit
floor
guest
key card
hall
lock
luggage
pocket
room
stairway
trolley

Others

toward (prep.)

Don put Sandra's luggage on a trolley...

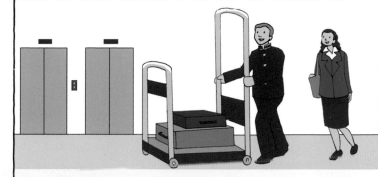

...and wheeled it toward the elevators.

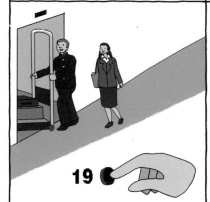

They boarded the elevator and Don pressed "19" for her floor.

They got off at the 19th floor.

Exit stairways are at this end of the hall and at the other end.

Don led the way to her room and pointed out the exits.

When they reached her room, Don pulled her key card from his pocket.

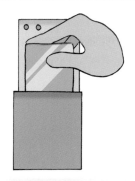

He inserted it into the lock...

...and opened the door.

Culture and Language

• *Lead the way* means "go first towards a place, with other people following you."

• In the United States, the ground floor is the 1st floor. In other countries, the 1st floor is the one above the ground floor. So, the 19th floor in the American system might be the 18th floor elsewhere.

11. Orienting a Guest to a Room

After opening the door,...

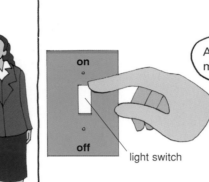

...Don turned on the room lights.

He motioned for Sandra to enter.

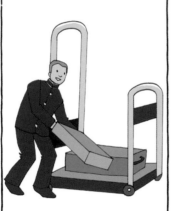

Don unloaded the bags from the trolley...

...and placed them near the luggage stand.

Then Don pulled the drapes open.

Then Don showed Sandra how to work the thermostat.

Sandra asked Don to turn up the air conditioning.

Then he showed Sandra the minibar.

coffeemaker

And here's the self-serve coffeemaker. It's complimentary, of course.

He pointed out the coffeemaker.

Then he opened the closet door...

pillow
blankets
shelf

You'll find extra pillows and blankets here if you need them.

...and mentioned that extra blankets and pillows were stored there.

To use this safe, follow the instructions on the door. Please secure your valuables here whenever you leave the room.

He also gave a brief introduction to using the in-room safe.

Those are the basics. Can I answer any questions for you?

No. Not now. I think I have it.

Finally, he asked if Sandra had any questions.

Well, if you have any questions at all later on, please don't hesitate to call the front desk.

He encouraged her to call the front desk any time if she had questions.

Thanks.

Thank you, ma'am.

She thanked him and gave him a tip.

Culture and Language

- To orient someone to a place is to teach them where things are located and how machines or systems work.
- *Drapes* are window coverings that reach almost to the floor. Another word for cloth window coverings is *curtains*. These may be shorter than drapes.

- *pull something open* = "pull something until it is open"
- *Turn something up* means "make something operate more forcefully." When you turn up an air conditioner, the room gets cooler. When you turn up the heat, the room gets warmer.

12. Showing the Guest How to Get Hotel Information

KEY VOCABULARY

Verbs

ask
contain
find [found]
look up
mention
open
point
point out
provide
require
say [said]
show
tell [told]

Nouns

back
channel
community
concierge
directory
entry
folder
hours
information
materials
list
resource
service
stationery

Adjectives

alphabetical
complimentary
open

How can I find out when things like the fitness center are open?

Channel 2 on your TV gives some information.

Sandra asked Don if there was a directory of hotel services.

HOTEL EVENTS

Don mentioned the hotel information channel on the TV.

But a more thorough list is in this folder.

He also showed Sandra the hotel-information folder.

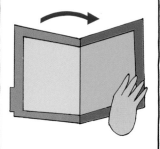

He opened the folder...

air conditioning
bar
bell services

...and pointed to the alphabetical list of services.

Fitness Center —daily 6 a.m. to 10 p.m. Guest card required for entry...

FITNESS CENTER
DAILY: 6 am to 10 pm
Guest card required for entry

Sandra looked up "fitness center" and found its hours.

And at the end you can see a list of banks, pizza places, churches, that sort of thing.

Don told her about the community directory at the back of the folder...

There are also some writing materials here.

...and pointed out that the folder also contained complimentary stationery.

If you have any questions during your stay, the concierge would be happy to answer them.

He said that the concierge could provide any other information about services or community resources.

Culture and Language

• *look something up* = find it in a book, on the Internet, or in some other resource

• *Stationery* means "letter paper, envelopes, and notepads."

13. Dealing with a Dissatisfied Guest

Verbs

agree
apologize
bother
call
complain
consult
deal [dealt] with
intervene
offer
reek
show
smell
take [took] care of
transfer

Nouns

cigarette smoke
computer
duty manager
front desk
inconvenience
office
room
smell
smoke
suite
upgrade

Adjectives

asthmatic
available
deluxe
different
dissatisfied
free
non-smoking
serious

Mr. Smith called the front desk to complain about his room.

Mr. Smith's family were dissatisfied because their room smelled like cigarette smoke.

The smell bothered their children, who were asthmatic.

Alberto's computer showed no available non-smoking rooms.

He consulted the duty manager, Maria.

Maria agreed to intervene.

Alberto transferred the call to Maria's office.

Maria found a non-smoking deluxe suite.

She offered the Smiths a free upgrade.

Maria showed Mr. Smith the new room...

...and apologized.

Culture and Language

- *Reek* means "give off a strong, usually unpleasant smell."
- *asthmatic* = having asthma, which is a kind of breathing problem

- *Dissatisfied* means "unhappy because something isn't good enough." The opposite is *satisfied*.
- *intervene* = get involved with someone else's problem

14. Checking in a Large Tour Group

KEY VOCABULARY

Verbs

check in
compare
distribute
get [got] off
give [gave]
go [went]
load
pull up
unload
wait

Nouns

bag
cargo hold
group
key
list
luggage trolley
reservation
roster
tour bus
tour guide

Others

entire (adj.)
first (adv.)
on behalf of (prep.)
outside (prep.)

A tour bus pulled up outside the hotel.

The tour guide got off the bus first...

...and went into the hotel.

The tour guide checked in on behalf of the entire group.

She and Alberto compared the group roster with the hotel's reservation list.

Alberto gave the tour guide all the keys.

A bellhop unloaded the bags from the cargo hold...

...and loaded them onto luggage trolleys.

The guide distributed the key cards.

Culture and Language

- *pull up* = "drive to a destination and stop there."
- *On behalf of* is a complex preposition meaning "as a representative of [someone else]."
- The opposite of *unload* is *load*.

- A bus's *cargo hold* is an area for luggage. It is usually a long area on the side of the bus. If it is at the back of a bus or car, it is called a "trunk."

15. Helping a Guest Ship a Parcel

KEY VOCABULARY

Verbs

calculate
charge
fill out
hand
inquire
send
ship

Nouns

account
address label
charge
copy
cost
delivery company
express service
label
parcel
package
service fee
tracking number

Adjectives

several
two-day

Sam inquired at the front desk about shipping a parcel.

The hotel has accounts with several parcel delivery companies.

He could send the package by airmail...

...or by two-day express service.

Sam filled out an address label to go with his package.

Alberto handed Sam a copy of the label with his tracking number.

The computer calculated the shipping charge plus the service fee.

Sam charged the cost to his room.

Culture and Language

- Types of shipping
  - air mail: transported by airplane
  - surface mail: transported by truck or train; slower than air mail
  - express: delivered very quickly. One type of express shipping is overnight—delivered the day after being sent.

- *parcel* = somewhat large piece of mail, e.g. a box. Parcels are usually wrapped in paper because they are too large for an envelope.
- A *tracking number* identifies a piece of mail sent by express. The number is used to find out where the item is —at its destination, at an airport, etc.

16. Parking a Guest's Car

Ms. Parin's car pulled up in front of the hotel.

Welcome to the Pine Ridge Hotel, ma'am.

After the driver's door opened, Teri held it open.

Don opened the passenger door...

...and unloaded luggage from the trunk.

Ms. Parin gave Teri her keys and a tip.

Teri got into the driver's seat.

She adjusted the seat and the rear-view mirror.

She buckled her seat belt...

...and put the car into drive.

PARKING FOR HOTEL GUESTS

She drove into the parking garage.

She turned the headlights on because the garage was dark.

VALET PARKING ONLY

She drove down a ramp toward the valet parking spaces.

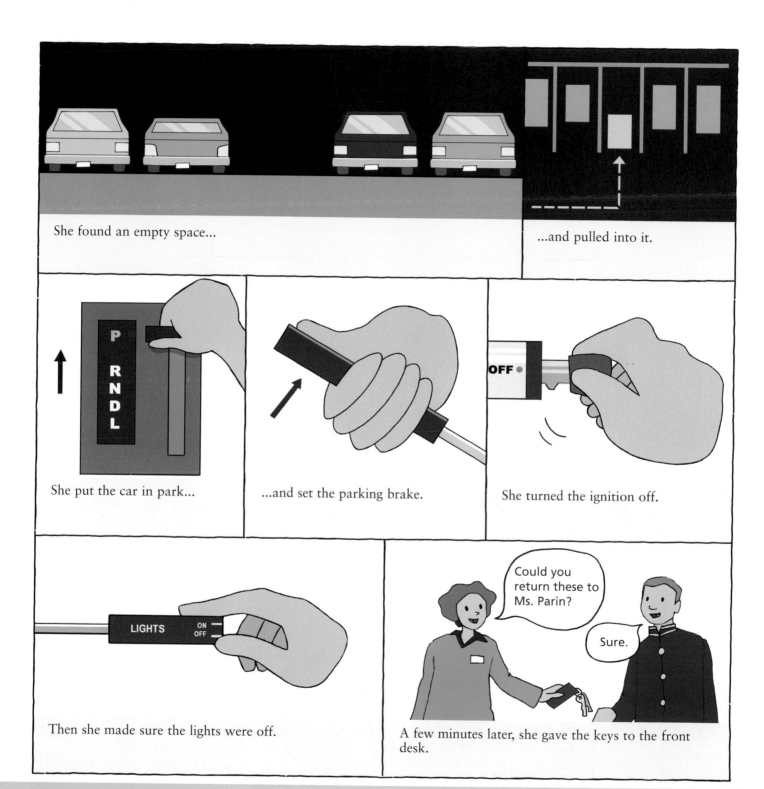

She found an empty space...

...and pulled into it.

She put the car in park...

...and set the parking brake.

She turned the ignition off.

Then she made sure the lights were off.

Could you return these to Ms. Parin?

Sure.

A few minutes later, she gave the keys to the front desk.

Culture and Language

- The guest tips the parking valet when giving her the keys because the guest will not see the valet later. The valet will give her keys to the front desk, which will pass them on to her.
- *Put the car into drive* means "select the 'D' setting so the car will move forward."

- Most hotels have parking spaces reserved for *valet parking*. This is a service in which hotel employees park a guest's car. Guests who park their own cars cannot park in these spaces.

17. Laundry Services 1: The Hotel Laundry

A pair of Maryn's pants had a stain on them.

She opened the closet...

...and took out the laundry bag.

She put the pants in the bag...

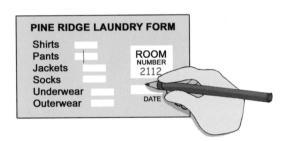

PINE RIDGE LAUNDRY FORM

Shirts
Pants
Jackets
Socks
Underwear
Outerwear

ROOM NUMBER
2112

DATE

...and filled out the laundry form.

She added the form to the bag of laundry.

2112

She left the bag outside her room.

That evening, Susan, the housekeeper, collected the dirty laundry.

Susan dropped off the clean clothes in the morning.

Clothes

jacket   top   dress   underwear   shirt   pants

28

18. Laundry Services 2: Coin-Operated Machines

Mr. Reynolds bought some detergent from a vending machine in the guest laundry.

He loaded his dirty clothes into the washing machine...

...and poured the detergent in.

He turned the temperature dial to select a warm wash...

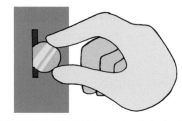

...and inserted coins in the coin slot.

Twenty minutes later, he took his wet clothes out of the washing machine.

He put them in the dryer.

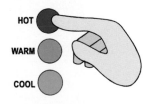

He chose the temperature...

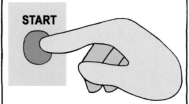

...and pushed the start button.

The dryer took one hour.

Mr. Reynolds unloaded his clean clothes from the dryer.

Culture and Language

- *to take one hour* = to need one hour's time to finish
- *temperature* = a measure of how hot or cold something is

- *Wet* clothes have a lot of water in them. *Dry* clothes do not.

19. Housekeeping 1: Dealing with Damage in a Room

KEY VOCABULARY

Verbs

call
deal [dealt] with
discover
file
fill out
find [found]
take [took] away
write [wrote]

Nouns

bar
bed
blanket
damage
desk
housekeeper
inventory
items
lamp
maintenance
manager
pillow
property
report
sheet
television (TV)

Adjectives

broken
damaged

Susan, a housekeeper, discovered damage in one of the rooms.

She called maintenance...

...and they took away the broken items.

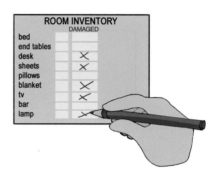

She filled out an inventory of damaged hotel property.

She wrote a report...

...and filed it with the hotel manager.

Culture and Language

- *fill out* vs. *file with*. To *fill out* a form is to write information on it. You *file* a form (or a report) *with* a supervisor by formally giving it to him or her.

- Members of the *maintenance* staff make repairs.
- An *inventory* is a list of everything in the room.

20. Housekeeping 2: Bringing Extra Amenities to the Room

Mr. Reynolds dialed "zero" to speak to the switchboard operator.

Front desk.

I'm trying to reach housekeeping, please.

He asked to be connected to housekeeping.

This is Mr. Reynolds in Room 1451.

He identified himself.

He asked for extra pillows.

He also needed a complimentary toothbrush.

I'll be right there.

The housekeeper offered to bring him the items.

1451

Housekeeping!

The housekeeper knocked on Mr. Reynolds's door.

Culture and Language

- *The housekeeper* is a person; *housekeeping* is the team of housekeepers.
- *I'll be right there* = I will come to you immediately.

- *dial zero* = to select "0" on a telephone's keypad. The verb *dial* means "turn a round control" on a machine. It is used for the action of selecting numbers on a telephone, even though the telephone's keypad is not round and is not turned.
- *complimentary* = free; at no charge

21. Housekeeping 3: Cleaning a Room

KEY VOCABULARY

Verbs

check (something) off
clean
disturb
dust
empty
enter
finish
make [made] the bed
open
replace
vacuum

Nouns

bathroom
carpet
clipboard
duster
master key
sponge
towel
vacuum cleaner
wastebasket

Adjectives

clean
dirty
unoccupied

Susan did not open this door.

She used her master key to enter an unoccupied room.

First, she cleaned the bathroom with a sponge.

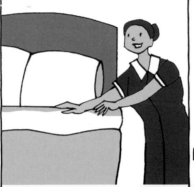

Then, she made the bed.

Next, she dusted the table with a duster.

After that, she emptied the wastebasket.

She replaced the dirty towels with clean towels.

Finally, she vacuumed the carpet with her vacuum cleaner.

When she had finished, she checked the room off on her clipboard.

Culture and Language

- A housekeeper never opens a door that has a "Do not disturb" sign on it. This sign means the guest is sleeping or busy and does not want anyone else to come in.

- A *master key* opens not just one door but many doors. Some hotels have master keys that open all the rooms in the whole hotel.

22. Room Service 1: Taking an Order

VOCABULARY

Verbs

answer
ask
confirm
dial
enter
estimate
have [had] dinner
identify oneself
order
quote
reach
want
would like

Nouns

beverage
Caesar salad
computer
delivery time
dinner
menu
mineral water
order
phone
price
room service
salad
size
tax

Ms. Parin wanted to have dinner in her room, so she dialed room service.

> Room service. How may I help you?

Cody answered the phone.

> Hello. This is Nancy Parin in room 819.

Nancy identified herself...

> I'd like a Caesar salad, please.

...and ordered a Caesar salad from the room service menu.

> Certainly ma'am. A large salad or just a side salad?

> A large salad, please. Large enough to be a dinner in itself.

Cody asked what size she would like.

> Right. A large Caesar salad.

Cody confirmed the order and entered it into the computer.

> Would you like anything else, ma'am? Some wine perhaps? Or some other beverage?

> I'll just have some mineral water, please.

He asked Nancy if she would like anything else.

> Thank you, ma'am. That will be $12.35 with tax. Your meal should reach you in about 30 minutes.

Cody quoted the price and estimated a delivery time.

Culture and Language

- *Order* food means "tell a waiter what food you would like."
- The noun *order* means "what you have told the waiter you would like."
- A *Caesar salad* usually includes lettuce, garlic, small dried fish, and a lemon-egg dressing.
- Cody asks if Nancy would like a beverage. A *beverage* is anything to drink—water, milk, a soft drink, wine, etc.
- *Would like* means "want to have."

23. Room Service 2: Delivering an Order

Cody put a clean tablecloth on a cart...

...and arranged food and some utensils on a tray that he put on the cart.

He wheeled the cart to her room.

He knocked on the door and identified himself when Nancy came to the door.

Yes?

Room service.

He took the tray of food off the cart and placed it on the coffee table.

He removed the covers from the food.

He opened her mineral water and poured it into a glass.

He ground some fresh pepper onto her salad.

He asked if everything was satisfactory.

Nancy asked if she could add some soup to the order.

Cody called the addition down to the kitchen.

Nancy signed for the meal.

Cody put the food covers on the cart...

...and walked toward the door.

Nancy thanked him and gave him a tip.

Culture and Language

- Cody put a tablecloth on the cart. This softens the appearance of the cart and makes it look something like a dinner table.
- *arrange* food = put containers of food into some kind of order
- *Utensils* for eating dinner include a knife, fork, and spoon.
- It is customary in North America for a waiter to *grind* fresh *black pepper* onto a salad if the customer wants it. The waiter might also put bits of fresh parmesan cheese on the salad at the customer's request.
- *satisfactory* = okay
- *To call an order down to the kitchen* means "to telephone the kitchen and place an order."
- Nancy *signs for* her meal. This means she puts her signature on the bill to add the meal charges to the amount she will pay when she checks out of the hotel.

24. Taking Messages for a Guest

Alberto answered the phone.

The caller asked for Ms. Parin.

Alberto asked the caller to wait a moment.

Alberto searched for Ms. Parin in the guest database.

Alberto tried to connect the caller to Ms. Parin's room...

...but Ms. Parin was out.

Alberto offered to take a message.

Alberto wrote down the message...

...and put a note in Ms. Parin's mailbox.

Culture and Language

- You *write down* small pieces of information you get from someone else.

- You *write* a letter, or a report, or other longer pieces.

25. Serving a Guest in the Gift Shop

Sam Monroe visited the hotel gift shop.

"Good morning. May I help you?"

The clerk offered to help him.

"I'm just looking at these postcards, thanks."

Mr. Monroe wanted to buy some postcards.

He picked out two postcards.

He also chose a present for his son.

The clerk rang up the purchases on the cash register.

17.50

Mr. Monroe paid in cash.

The clerk gave him his change.

Culture and Language

- You *ring up* a purchase when you enter the cost of items in the register.
- *Cash* is money (paper money and coins).

- *Change* is money you get back if you give a clerk more than the cost of an item.

26. The Guest's Experience: Signing for Drinks and Snacks

KEY VOCABULARY

Verbs

ask
catch [caught]
go [went]
leave [left]
order
sign
sign for

Nouns

attention
bar
bartender
check
glass
peanuts
room number
snack
tip
whiskey

Mr. Porter went to the hotel bar.

He caught the bartender's attention.

Could I have some peanuts?

Mr. Porter ordered a glass of whiskey.

He also asked for a snack.

The bartender left the check with Mr. Porter.

Mr. Porter wrote his room number on the check and signed it.

Then he left a tip for the bartender.

Culture and Language

- The *check* is sometimes called "the bill."
- When Mr. Porter wrote his room number on the bill, he *charged it to his room.*

- Mr. Porter gives the bartender a *tip*—extra money to thank him for his service.

27. The Guest's Experience: Using the Business Center

Ms. Randall went to the hotel's business center.

She logged on to the computer with her room number.

She checked her e-mail.

She searched for some information on the Internet.

She did some word processing...

...and printed a document out.

She photocopied the document...

...and then sent a fax to her office.

Culture and Language

- *Check your e-mail* means "see if you have any messages."
- *Word processing* is writing with a computer.

- *search for* = try to find

28. The Guest's Experience: In-Room Entertainment

KEY VOCABULARY

Verbs

adjusted
change
choose [chose]
play
press
turn on
turn off
watch

Nouns

button
channel
guide
kids
menu
movie
remote control
television (TV)
video game
volume

Others

pay-per-view (adj.)
together (adv.)

Mr. Reynolds turned on the television.

He changed the channel...

...and he adjusted the volume.

Then the kids played a video game.

Mrs. Reynolds read the TV guide.

She pressed the menu button.

The family chose a pay-per-view movie.

They all watched the movie together.

Then Mr. Reynolds turned off the TV.

Culture and Language

- When you watch a *pay-per-view* movie, a charge is added to your hotel bill.

- *adjust the volume* = change the loudness until it is just right

29. The Guest's Experience: Using the Family Pool

KEY VOCABULARY

KEY VOCABULARY

Verbs

ask
climb
dive [dove]
dry oneself
get [got] out
relax
swim [swam]
watch

Nouns

armband
changing rooms
daughter
end
lap
step
swimming pool
swimsuit
towel
whirlpool

Adjectives

afloat
deep
shallow

The Karini family asked for pool towels at the front desk.

They went into the changing rooms...

...and changed into their swimsuits.

Mr. Karini dove into the pool.

Mrs. Karini put armbands on her daughter to help her stay afloat.

Her son climbed down the steps at the shallow end of the pool.

Mrs. Karini relaxed in the whirlpool.

Mr. Karini swam laps.

They all got out of the pool...

...and dried themselves with their towels.

Culture and Language

- A family pool is one where children and adults can play. The hotel might also have another pool just for exercise, called a lap pool.
- When you *swim laps*, you swim up and down the length of the pool for exercise.

- The past tense of *dive* is *dove* (with a long "o"), but some people use "dived" instead.
- *shallow* = not deep
- A *whirlpool* is a very small, shallow pool with very warm water and constant jets of water shooting into the pool from the sides.

30. The Guest's Experience: Using the Fitness Center
1 - In the Gym

Sandra went to the fitness center to work out.

To warm up, she did some stretches.

Verbs

cool down
dive [dove]
do [did] (an exercise)
dry off
get [got] dressed
get [got] out
go [went]
hang [hung]
lift weights
put [put] on
ride [rode]
run [ran]
swim [swam]
take [took] a shower
warm up
work out

Nouns

aerobic exercise
exercise
fitness center
gym
lap pool
locker
locker room
pool
shower
stair-stepper
stationary bike
street clothes
stretch
swimsuit
towel
treadmill
upper-body strength
weights

Then she did some aerobic exercises by riding a stationary bike...

...using a stair-stepper...

...and running on a treadmill.

For upper-body strength, she lifted weights.

She cooled down...

...and then went back to her room to take a shower.

Culture and Language

- *Aerobic exercise* improves your breathing, the efficiency of your heart, and your body's ability to get oxygen.

- *Upper-body strength* is the strength of your arms, your shoulders, and your back.
- *stationary* = not moving

2 - At the Lap Pool

Sam Monroe went to the locker room by the pool...

...and put his swimsuit on.

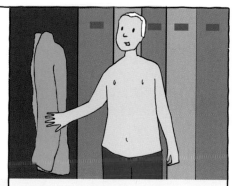

He hung his street clothes in a locker.

 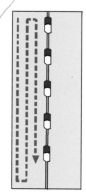

He dove into the pool and swam some laps.

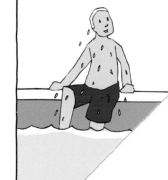

After he got out of the pool, he dried himself off with a towel.

Back at the locker room, he took a shower...

...and got dressed.

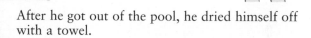

- You *take a shower* or *take a bath* to get clean.

- *Street clothes* are the clothes people usually wear. They are different from gym clothes or exercise clothes or swimwear.

31. The Guest's Experience: At the Executive Lounge
1 - In the Evening

KEY VOCABULARY

KEY VOCABULARY

Verbs

ask
eat [ate]
check out
enjoy
give [gave]
help oneself
look
order
set [set]
set up
sit [sat]
sit [sat] down
start
take [took]

Nouns

armchair
attendant
bar
buffet
cocktail hour
coffee
cook
cup
executive lounge
food
hors d'oeuvres
hostess
rack
reception desk
refill
service desk
table
view
window

Adjectives

self-service
small

EXECUTIVE LOUNGE

"Welcome, sir. Which room number?"

"I'm in 204."

At the reception desk in the executive lounge, Sam gave his room number to the hostess.

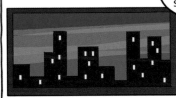

He took a newspaper off the rack...

...and sat down in an armchair near the window.

He looked out the window...

...and enjoyed a view of the city.

"Ladies and gentlemen, you're all welcome to have cocktails and some snacks if you'd like."

At 6:00, the cocktail hour started.

The attendants set up a buffet of hors d'oeuvres...

...and a small self-service bar.

Culture and Language

- If you *sit down* somewhere, you go from a standing position to a sitting position. If you *sit* somewhere, you simply stay there in a sitting position.

- If you *help yourself* to something, you take some of it by yourself, without anyone else serving you. This is a *self-service* system.

2 - In the Morning

There was a breakfast buffet in the lounge.

Sam ordered an omelet from the cook...

> Could I have an omelet? Cheese, tomato, and green pepper, please.

...and asked one of the attendants for a cup of coffee.

> Could I just have some coffee, please? With milk.

He took some fruit and some pastries from the buffet...

...and sat at the table to eat his breakfast.

While Sam got a refill of his coffee,...

> Should I top that off for you, sir?

...another guest checked out of the hotel at the service desk in the lounge.

> I'd like to check out, please.

- *Cup of* often comes before *coffee* or *tea*. It is not an exact measurement, just a phrase that allows you to count servings of the drink: <u>one</u> *cup of coffee*, <u>two</u> *cups of coffee*, etc.

- In a *buffet*, several items of food are set out in a line on a long table. The guests take turns going past the food items and taking whatever they want.
- An *hors d'oeuvre* is a snack item. It is pronounced *or-DERV*.

32. Taking a Restaurant Reservation by Phone

Good afternoon. The Grill Room Restaurant. How may I help you?

Emma answered the phone.

Yes. Hello. My name is Mike Gordon. I'd like to make a reservation for the evening...

The caller asked for a reservation later in the day...

There are four of us, and we'd like a table at about 7:00.

...and gave some details about the time and the size of the party.

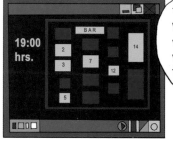

Yes, Mr. Gordon. We have some very nice window tables for four at 7:00.

Emma checked the reservation log on her computer.

She told the caller that a table for four was available then.

Would you like smoking or non?

She asked about his seating preferences...

It's my wife's birthday. Could you put a bouquet of a dozen red roses on the table?

Certainly, Mr. Gordon. We'll just add that to your bill.

...and he requested a special service.

19:00 hrs
GORDON
non-smoking
window

place 12 red roses on table before seating guests.

Emma noted the request...

So we'll see you at 7:00 this evening, Mr. Gordon. The roses will be on the table before you're seated.

Thank you very much. Bye.

...and confirmed the details of the reservation.

Culture and Language

- A *party of four* means a group of four people.
- A *log* is a list.
- Mr. Gordon's request for special service involves an expensive item.

A *dozen* (12) roses could cost as much as $80. The restaurant cannot afford to *comp* them—give them to him for free.

33. Accommodating Guests Who Have No Reservation

Ms. Lopez walked up to the hostess station.

Emma, the hostess, asked her if she had a reservation.

Emma asked for the number of people in Ms. Lopez's party.

She needed a table for six.

Emma checked the waiting list...

...and estimated the wait for a table.

She took Ms. Lopez's name...

...and suggested that she wait in the bar.

Culture and Language

- To *walk up to* something is to walk towards it until you are very near.

- *estimate* = guess about an amount
- *take* (someone's) *name* = write the name on a list

34. Explaining That No Table Is Available

Mr. and Mrs. Reynolds went to the hotel restaurant.

They hadn't reserved a table.

There were no tables available...

...and the waiting list was very long.

Mrs. Reynolds could not wait.

The hostess showed them a list of other local restaurants.

They chose a nearby Italian restaurant.

The hostess called the Italian restaurant for them.

Culture and Language

- If you *reserve a table*, you ask the restaurant to hold it open for you at a certain time.

- Italian restaurants serve food from Italy, such as spaghetti and pizza.

35. Seating Guests

KEY VOCABULARY

Verbs

check
enjoy
find [found]
give [gave]
hold [held]
lead [led]
offer
pick up
wish

Nouns

chair
list
meal
menu
reservation
seating chart
table
wine list

Adjective

pleasant

Emma, the hostess, checked the Porters' name on her reservation list.

Right. Here we are.

She found their table on the seating chart.

She picked up two menus...

...and led the Porters to their table.

She held the chair for Mrs. Porter.

Emma gave them menus...

Haute Chousou

bottle $25.00
half $14.00

...and offered Mr. Porter the wine list.

Enjoy your meal.

She wished them a pleasant meal.

Culture and Language

- *wish* (someone) *a pleasant meal* = say you hope the person enjoys his or her food

- A *menu* lists food you can order. A *wine list* is usually separate from the menu.

36. Taking a Beverage Order and Serving Beverages

KEY VOCABULARY

Verbs

fill an order
introduce oneself
leave [left]
place
pour
refill
return
set [set]
set [set] down
take [took] an order

Nouns

bar
bartender
beer
beverage
bottle
drink
glass
orange juice
order
rock
server
table
tray
water

Adjectives

light
one's own

Katie introduced herself...

...and took their beverage order.

She poured two glasses of water and walked the beverage order up to the bar.

The bartender filled Katie's beverage order for her.

...and she returned to the table with a tray of drinks.

She placed Mr. Porter's bottle of beer on the table and set a beer glass next to it.

He poured his own beer while Katie gave Mrs. Porter her orange juice.

Before she left, she refilled their water glasses.

Culture and Language

- A *beverage* is a drink.
- A *drink* may be alcoholic (beer, wine, etc.) or non-alcoholic (water, juice, etc.).
- *take an order* = write down what a customer wants

- In North American restaurants, a *bartender* often gives the servers any drink that the customer orders, even non-alcoholic drinks.
- *Set* means "put in a place." *Set down* means "put something—which you have been carrying—onto a surface."

37. Taking a Meal Order

Katie checked that the Porters were ready to order.

She wrote the table number, the number of guests, and her server number on the check.

First, she took Mrs. Porter's order.

Then Mr. Porter ordered his entrée.

She asked Mr. Porter how he liked his steak cooked.

Katie wrote down the order on the check.

She took their menus...

...and put the order in to the kitchen.

Culture and Language

• If you order an *entrée*, it means the main dish of a meal in the U. S., but at very formal meals in the U. K., *entrée* is a small dish served just before the main part

• Menu is a list of the food that you can eat in a restaurant: If you eat *à la carte*, you choose each dish from a separate list instead of eating a fixed combination of dishes at a fixed price.

38. Serving Food

KEY VOCABULARY

Verbs

be [was] up
bring [brought]
call
carry
check
enjoy
load
offer
say [said]
serve
set [set] down
wish

Nouns

basket
bread
chef
dinner salad
entrée
lobster
meal
plate
sauce
stand
tray

Adjectives

all right
fold-out
pleasant
ready

Katie brought dinner salads and a basket of bread to the Porters' table.

She said that their entrées would be ready soon.

The chef called that the Porters' order was up.

Katie loaded the plates onto a tray.

She carried the tray and a fold-out stand to the Porters' table.

She set the tray down on the stand.

She served the entrées.

Katie checked to see that everything was all right...

...and wished them a pleasant meal.

Culture and Language

- The entrées that the Porters ordered come with dinner salads. The Porters get them without having to order them separately. The basket of bread is given to every table where an order is taken. The guests can get refills on the bread.

- An *entrée* is the main dish in an order.

39. Serving Wine

KEY VOCABULARY

Verbs

approve
bring [brought]
check
hand
hold [held]
pour
pull out
read
remove
screw
taste

Nouns

amount
bottle
cork
corkscrew
foil
glass
label
middle
top
wine

Adjective

small

Katie brought the Porters' bottle of wine to their table.

That looks right.

She held the bottle for Mr. Porter so he could read the label.

corkscrew

She pulled out her corkscrew and removed the foil from the top of the bottle.

Katie screwed the corkscrew into the middle of the cork...

...and pulled the cork out.

Hmmm. Looks fine to me.

She handed the cork to Mr. Porter so he could check it.

Then she poured a small amount into his wine glass so he could taste it.

Oh, yes. This tastes really good.

He approved...

...so Katie poured glasses of wine for the Porters.

Culture and Language

• Mr. Porter *tastes* the wine. Some people also smell it and swirl it around in the glass before they approve it.

• *approve* = to say something is right or acceptable

40. Taking Dessert and Coffee Orders

KEY VOCABULARY

Verbs

bring [brought]
clear
collect
get out of
give [gave]
offer
order
pour

Nouns

cheesecake
coffee
dessert
fork
menu
plate
server station
silverware

Adjective

decaffeinated

Katie cleared the plates and silverware.

She gave the Porters dessert menus.

Mrs. Porter didn't want a dessert...

...but Mr. Porter ordered the cheesecake.

Katie offered them coffee...

...and poured a cup of decaffeinated coffee for Mrs. Porter.

She collected a fork from the server station...

...and brought Mr. Porter's cheesecake.

Culture and Language

- Mrs. Porter says she is *full* because she has had enough to eat.

- *Decaffeinated* coffee—also called *decaf*—is coffee without caffeine, the chemical that keeps you awake. Coffee with caffeine is called *regular* coffee.

41. Taking Payment at the Table

KEY VOCABULARY

Verbs

add
bring [brought]
enter
give [gave]
hand to
key
print
read [read]
sign
signal
swipe
take [took] out

Nouns

amount
bill
bottom line
cash
charge
computer
credit card
folder
merchant's copy
order
pen
reader
register
slip
tip
waitress

Mr. Porter signaled to the waitress to bring the bill.

Katie keyed the order in at the register.

The computer printed the bill.

Katie put the bill in a folder...

I'll take this whenever you are ready.

...and handed it to Mr. Porter.

Mr. Porter read the bill...

...and took out his credit card.

He gave the card and bill to the waitress.

Culture and Language

- In American English, the *bill* is often called the "check."
- A *folder* is a cover to contain pieces of paper. It opens up like a book.
- In the United States, restaurant customers are expected to leave a tip—extra money for the waitress or waiter—equal to 15 percent to 20 percent of the bill's amount.

When they pay by credit card, they write the amount of the tip on the credit-card slip.
- Credit card slips contain at least two sheets of paper—a white merchant's copy and a yellow customer's copy.

Katie entered the amount of the bill into the credit card reader...

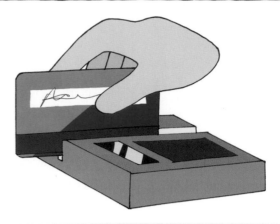

...and swiped Mr. Porter's credit card through the reader.

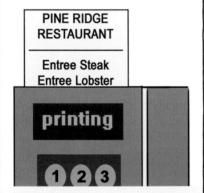

The reader printed a credit card slip.

Katie gave Mr. Porter the charge slip and a pen.

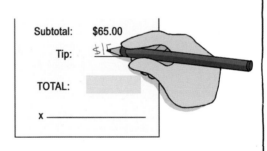

Mr. Porter added a tip...

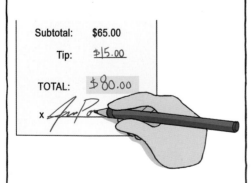

...and signed on the bottom line.

Katie took the merchant's copy...

...and put it in the cash register.

42. Taking Payment at a Register 1: A Satisfied Customer

KEY VOCABULARY

Verbs

ask
enter
give [gave]
hand
leave [left]
pay [paid]
return
say [said] goodbye
take [took]
thank

Nouns

amount
bill
cash
cashier
change
cheek
credit card
form of payment
register
tip

Adverb

in cash

Mr. Reynolds took his bill to the cashier.

He handed the bill to Emma,...

...who entered the amount in the cash register.

Cash, check, or credit card?

She asked Mr. Reynolds which form of payment he was using.

I'll pay cash.

Mr. Reynolds chose to pay in cash.

Okay. Out of 30. Here's 18, 19, 20, and 30.

Emma gave him his change.

Mr. Reynolds returned to the table to leave a tip.

Thank you!

Emma thanked Mr. Reynolds and said goodbye.

Culture and Language

- Payment at the cash register is common at coffee shops, snack bars, and other informal restaurants.

- When Emma gives Mr. Porter his change, she "counts it back" to him. This is the polite way to make sure you are giving the correct amount of change.

43. Taking Payment at a Register 2: A Dissatisfied Customer

KEY VOCABULARY

Verbs

apologize
charge
complain
contact
dry
enjoy
go [went]
inform
overcook
remove
write [wrote]

Nouns

cashier
check
chef
customer
entrée
manager
meal
problem
quality
total

Adjective

unhappy

Sandra Randall did not enjoy her meal.

She went to the cashier.

Excuse me. I'm not at all happy with my meal. My chicken was dry and overcooked.

She complained about the quality of her meal.

The cashier contacted the restaurant manager.

I'm very sorry, ma'am.

The manager apologized.

Let me remove that charge from your bill.

~~Entree~~
~~Chicken Special~~
~~$12.99~~

Beverage
Cola large

The manager didn't charge Sandra for her entrée.

Thank you for your understanding.

Sandra wrote a check for the new total.

Edward, we had a very unhappy customer.

The manager informed the chef about the problem.

Culture and Language

• *complain* = say that something is wrong and that you're unhappy about it

• The *chef* supervises the kitchen and all the cooks.

44. Taking Payment at a Register 3: A Credit Card Problem

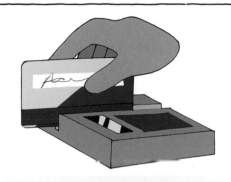

Emma, the cashier, swiped Sam Monroe's credit card through the card reader.

However, the machine rejected the card.

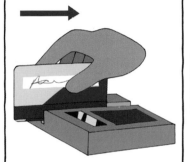

Emma retried the card...

...but the transaction failed again.

> I'm sorry, sir. This card is not working for some reason.

Emma handed the card back to Sam.

> Oh. My mistake. This one has expired.

Sam realized that his card had expired.

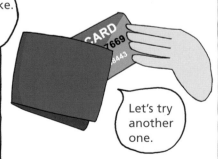

> Let's try another one.

Sam took out a different card.

The machine accepted the new card.

KEY VOCABULARY

Verbs

accept
completed
expire
fail
hand back
realize
reject
retry
swipe
take [took] out
work

Nouns

cashier
credit card
error
machine
mistake
reader
reason
transaction

Others

again (adv.)
different (adj.)
new (adj.)

Culture and Language

- *Reject* is the opposite of *accept*.

- A card that has *expired* is past the time during which it can work.

45. Explaining the Details of a Hotel Tour

Verbs

describe
eat
explain
give [gave]
go along
reserve
stop
travel
wonder

Nouns

boxed lunch
coach
concierge
guide
museum
park
place
route
sights
ticket
tour

Adjective

historic

Sandra Randall asked about the hotel's tours.

Paul, the concierge, explained the route of the tour.

He said they would travel by coach.

A guide would describe the sights of the city.

They would stop at the museum...

...and eat a boxed lunch in the park.

Ms. Randall reserved her place on the tour.

The concierge gave her a ticket.

Culture and Language

- A *boxed lunch* is a take-out meal that could include sandwiches, chips, fruit, and a drink.
- A *concierge* helps hotel guests get dinner reservations, arrange transportation, find their way around town, etc.
- *sights of the city* = interesting places in the city
- This chapter uses *would* to indicate activities that *might* happen if Sandra takes the tour.

46. Advising Guests about Nearby Restaurants

KEY VOCABULARY

Verbs

ask
catch
check
give [gave]
hurry
look for
show

Nouns

bus schedule
concierge
list
location
map
mile
taxi
watch

Adjective

local

Mr. Smith asked the concierge about local restaurants.

The concierge showed him a list of some.

Mr. Smith was looking for a Mexican restaurant.

The concierge showed him the location of a restaurant on a map...

...and gave him a bus schedule.

Mr. Smith checked his watch...

...and hurried out of the hotel...

...to catch the bus.

Culture and Language

• *catch a bus* = get on a bus

• Restaurants are often identified by a type of national cuisine, such as Mexican, Italian, or Thai.

47. Arranging for a Taxi and Courtesy Car

KEY VOCABULARY

Verbs

arrive
ask
book
call
go [went]
open
put [put]
require
speak [spoke]

Nouns

airport
concierge
courtesy car
door
downtown
driver
suitcases
taxi
trunk

Adverb

outside

Mrs. Porter called the concierge to book a taxi.

Paul, the concierge, asked her what time she required the taxi.

Paul called for a taxi.

Then, the Reynolds family came to the concierge desk.

They needed a courtesy car to the airport.

Paul went outside to speak to the courtesy car driver.

He opened the car door...

...and put the suitcases in the trunk.

Culture and Language

- A *courtesy car* offers no-cost transportation to hotel guests.
- To *book* a taxi is to arrange for one to pick you up.

48. Booking the Hotel for Future Conferences

KEY VOCABULARY

Verbs

book
check
explain
fill in
give [gave]
go [went]
include
pencil in
take [took] out

Nouns

booking form
business card
calendar
conference
details
event planner
lodging
nature
price
quote
request

Sandra Randall went to see the hotel's event planner, Beatriz Chan.

She gave her business card to Beatriz...

...and explained the nature of her request.

Beatriz checked her calendar...

...and penciled in Sandra's conference.

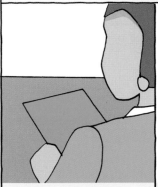

Beatriz took out a booking form...

...and filled in the details of the conference.

Finally, she gave Sandra a price quote.

Culture and Language

- *Pencil in* means "make a temporary arrangement for."

- A *quote* is an estimate of the total cost.

63

49. Directing Guests to Facilities Near the Hotel

KEY VOCABULARY

Verbs

ask
circle
explore
get [got] off
give [gave]
go [went] jogging
go [went] sight-seeing
head
mark
point out
show

Nouns

area
information
leaflet
map
path
route
sight-seeing
station
street map
subway
system

Adjective

nearest

Mrs. Porter wanted to go jogging.

Paul showed her a street map of the area.

Then you can head east again on the Cold Creek path.

I'd like to explore the area. Any ideas?

There is a lot to see, sir. This lists some popular spots.

He marked a route on the map.

Mr. Porter asked about sightseeing.

The concierge gave him an information leaflet...

...and a map of the subway system.

You'll get off at Carbury Street. That's near a lot of things.

He circled the station where Mr. Porter would get off...

...and pointed him toward the nearest station.

Culture and Language

- *Jogging* is a relaxed form of running.
- *sightseeing* = going to interesting or famous places in an area

- A *subway* may also be called: *the trains, the metro, the underground* or some abbreviation of the system's name, e.g., *the MRT* for "the Mass Rapid Transit system."

50. Handling a Request for Child Care

KEY VOCABULARY

Verbs

answer
arrange
book
confirm
decide
explain
find out
mention
need
provide
reassure
say [said]
specify
suggest
worried

Nouns

alternative
babysitter
booking
call
charge
child care
front desk
license
quality
split
state

Adjectives

available
dependable
free
nominal

Concierge.

Hi. We need to find a babysitter tonight for our two children.

Paul answered a call from Mr. Reynolds about child care.

We have a free child care center — our Kids' Club — until 7:30 in the evening.

Paul mentioned the free child care that the hotel provides.

Yes, I heard about that from the front desk. I'm afraid we'll be out much later, from 6:00 to about 10:00.

Mr. Reynolds said he needed something later than that.

Yes, we have several on-call people available tonight. Would you like to book someone from 6 until 10?

Then perhaps one of our on-call child care workers would be available. Let me check...

Paul suggested an alternative.

CHILD CARE

He found out that a childcare worker would be available.

Are they dependable? What qualifications do they have?

They have to have a license from the state to work for us, sir. They are very good.

Mr. Reynolds was worried about the quality of the child care, and Paul reassured him.

There is a nominal fee, sir. These child care workers charge $10, but the guest and the hotel split that. You would pay $5 an hour, and the hotel would match it.

Paul explained the charges.

Sounds good. Could you send the sitter up to Room 1451 by six? We'd need someone to stay until 10 or 10:30.

Mr. Reynolds decided to book someone.

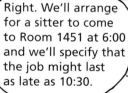

Right. We'll arrange for a sitter to come to Room 1451 at 6:00 and we'll specify that the job might last as late as 10:30.

Great. Thank you.

Paul confirmed the booking and said he would arrange things.

Culture and Language

- The term *child care worker* is a little more acceptable than *babysitter*. The children they care for are often too old to be called "babies."

- *reassure* = make someone feel less worried or uncertain

51. Lost and Found

KEY VOCABULARY

KEY VOCABULARY

Verbs

approach
ask
bring [brought]
describe
explain
hand over
happen
pick out
put
say [said]
take [took]
walk

Nouns

box
concierge desk
front desk
lost and found
plaid pattern
umbrella

Someone left an umbrella in the restaurant.

Katie brought it to the concierge desk and explained what happened.

Paul took it to the front desk and asked them to put it in the lost-and-found.

Later, Sandra Randall approached Paul to ask about the umbrella.

Paul walked with her to the front desk.

She described the umbrella.

Pat went back to the lost-and-found box and picked out the umbrella.

Sandra said that it was hers...

...so Pat handed it over to her.

Culture and Language

- Usually, lost items are kept behind the front desk for security reasons. Some hotels have a box for these items. Others have a whole storage room for them.

- The term *lost-and-found* usually means a place. Sometimes, it might also mean the group of objects in that place.

52. Helping a Guest Who Is Injured

Mr. Porter was taking the stairs to the lobby...

when he tripped...

...and fell down the stairs.

Help!

He called for help.

Let me help you, sir. Are you injured?

Maria heard the noise.

I think I did something to my ankle.

Mr. Porter said where he was injured.

Right. Let's take it easy and not move too much. Here, let me put this cushion under your head.

Maria tried to make Mr. Porter comfortable and keep him from moving.

We have an injured guest at the Pine Ridge Hotel. Please get a crew here right away.

She called the emergency services...

...and soon an ambulance arrived.

Culture and Language

- *take the stairs* = use the stars to get somewhere
- If you *trip*, you start falling because your foot gets caught on something while you are walking.

- When a guest is injured, he or she should not be moved any more than necessary. Movement could make the injury worse.

53. Getting Medical Care for a Guest

KEY VOCABULARY

Verbs

call around
explain
feel [felt] sick
have [had]
suggest
take to

Nouns

cough
doctor
emergency room
(ER)
fever
hospital
problem
urgent care clinic

Others

bad (adj.)
on call (adv.)

Mrs. Reynolds' son, Brian, was feeling sick.

He had a fever...

...and a bad cough.

Mrs. Reynolds called the front desk.

It's my son...

She explained the problem to Pat.

EMERGENCY

We could take him to the emergency room at Barton Hospital...

Pat suggested taking Brian to the E.R...

URGENT CARE CLINIC +

...or to one of the clinics near here.

...or to an urgent care clinic.

No, I don't think he should go anywhere. Can we get a doctor to come here?

Mrs. Porter wanted a doctor to see Brian.

DOCTORS

Pat called around to find a doctor who was on call.

Culture and Language

- The *emergency room* is a department in a hospital. If you need to see a doctor, but are not seriously ill, you can go to an *urgent care clinic* instead.

- A doctor who is *on call* is available outside normal office hours.
- *call around* = call many different places

54. Dealing with Noisy Guests

KEY VOCABULARY

Verbs

apologize
bang
call
disturb
explain
knock
lower
open
report
sleep [slept]
stop
turn down

Nouns

front desk
guest
midnight
noise
television (TV)
volume
wall

Others

late (adv.)
next door (adv.)
noisy (adj.)

Mr. Monroe couldn't sleep because of the noise next door.

He banged on the wall, but the noise didn't stop.

Mr. Monroe called the front desk and reported the noise.

Alberto knocked on the door of the noisy guests.

A man opened the door.

Alberto asked him to turn down the volume on the television.

He explained that it was late.

The man apologized and lowered the TV volume.

Culture and Language

- When guests speak with a hotel employee on the telephone, they should not be put on hold for longer than fifteen seconds. If a hotel staff member offers to call back with information, the follow-up call should be made within ten minutes.

55. Advising a Guest About Safe Storage

KEY VOCABULARY

Verbs

ask
call
fill out
fit [fit]
keep
store
suggest
take [took]

Nouns

briefcase
combination lock
contents
description
documents
front desk
passport
safe
suggestion
valuables

Adjective

secure

Mr. Monroe called the front desk to ask about keeping his briefcase secure.

He kept important documents, his passport, and some other valuables in his briefcase.

The clerk suggested the safe in the room...

...with a combination lock.

But the briefcase didn't fit in the safe.

On Pat's suggestion, he took his valuables to the front desk.

At the front desk, he filled out a description of the contents of his briefcase.

Alberto stored the briefcase in the hotel safe.

Culture and Language

- *Combination locks* open if you put in the correct series of numbers.
- *secure* = safe

- *contents* = things inside
- *valuables* = important or expensive things you own

56. The Guest's Experience: Reporting a Problem

KEY
KEY VOCABULARY

Verbs

call
complete
dial
find [found]
fix
go [went]
mop up
report
return

Nouns

bathroom
floor
department
leak
maintenance
problem
report
water
worker
zero

Others

flooded (adj.)
immediately (adv.)

The Porters returned to their room and found water on the floor.

Mr. Porter dialed "zero" to call the front desk.

My bathroom is flooded!

Mr. Porter reported the problem to Alberto.

MAINTENANCE REPORT

Alberto completed a maintenance report...

Maintenance?

...and called the maintenance department.

222

A maintenance worker went immediately to the Porters' room.

He fixed the leak...

...and mopped up the water.

Culture and Language

- *Report* can be a verb (*he reported the problem*) or a noun (*he wrote a report*).

- In most hotels, dialing "O" (zero) will connect you to the front desk.
- *fix something* = make it work again after it was broken

57. The Guest's Experience: Getting Ready to Leave the Hotel

KEY VOCABULARY

Verbs

call
check
close
come [came]
get [got] ready
leave [left]
load
pack
pick up
take [took]

Nouns

bathroom
bellhop
closet
clothes
drawer
room keys
suitcase
toiletries
trolley

Maryn packed her clothes into her suitcases.

She took her toiletries from the bathroom.

She closed the suitcases...

...and called the front desk.

A bellhop came to her room...

...and loaded the suitcases onto a trolley.

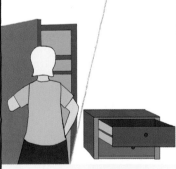

She checked the closet and the drawers...

and picked up the room keys.

Culture and Language

• At most hotels, check-out time is 12:00 noon. Some hotels may offer a later check-out option at no charge, but most hotels charge an additional fee for late check-out. Guests should arrange for late check-out with the front desk in advance.

58. Checking a Guest Out:
A Dispute about the Bill

KEY VOCABULARY

Verbs

cancel
charge
check
check out
dispute
find [found]
print out
show
sign

Nouns

amount
bill
charge
credit card
express checkout
local call
problem
service directory

Adverb

ready

The night clerk slipped Ms. Lopez's express checkout bill under her door.

Ms. Lopez checked the bill...

...and found a problem.

When she was ready to check out, she showed the bill to Pat.

- Room Service: $32.00
- Local telephone call: $4.50

She disputed the charge for a local call.

Telephone Services

Pat showed Ms. Lopez the fees in the service directory.

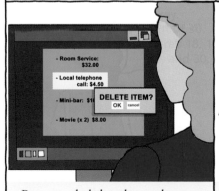

- Room Service: $32.00
- Local telephone call: $4.50
- Mini-bar: $1...
- Movie (x 2) $8.00

DELETE ITEM? OK cancel

Pat canceled the phone charge...

...and printed out a new bill.

card #: 1368·221·741
X

Ms. Lopez signed to charge the new amount to her credit card.

Culture and Language

- In *express checkout*, the bill is delivered under the room door. If it is correct, the guest does not have to stop at the front desk before leaving the hotel.

- disPUTE (verb; stress on the 2nd syllable) = to say [something] is not correct
- DISpute (noun; stress on the 1st syllable) = a disagreement

59. Exchanging Currency

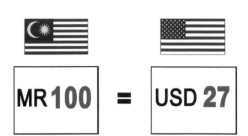

At check-out, Sandra asked about getting some foreign currency.

The posted exchange rates showed that she could exchange US$27 for 100 ringgit.

She was paying with her traveler's checks, so Rob asked to see her passport.

He filled in some fields in the automatic currency converter...

...and entered the amount of the traveler's checks.

Sandra countersigned the checks.

Rob counted out Sandra's money...

...and gave it to her along with her passport.

Culture and Language

- The name of Malaysia's currency is the *ringgit*, just as the name of the US currency is the dollar.

- When you buy travelers checks from a bank, you sign them. When you cash a check, you sign it a second time (countersign).

60. Storing Luggage after Check-Out

KEY VOCABULARY

Verbs

ask
check out
enjoy
fill in
give [gave]
leave [left]
put [put]
store

Nouns

bellhop
claim check
date
flight
luggage
luggage check
name
tags

Adjective

several

Maryn Karini and her family were checking out...

...but they still had several hours before their flight.

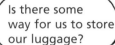

They asked to leave their luggage at the hotel.

Pat gave Maryn some luggage tags.

Maryn filled in her name and the date.

The bellhop put the suitcases in the hotel's luggage check.

He gave Maryn the claim checks.

Maryn and her family left to enjoy their day.

Culture and Language

- *Suitcase* is a count noun (*She has many suitcases.*). *Luggage* is a non-count, mass noun and refers to all the suitcases and other things one is carrying. (*She has a lot of luggage.*)

- *have several hours before X* = be several hours earlier than the time when X happens

75

61. The Guest's Experience: Leaving the Hotel

KEY
KEY VOCABULARY

Verbs

arrive
check
check out
drop
enjoy
fill out
leave [left]
wait
write [wrote]

Nouns

airport
box
comment
comment card
questionnaire
shuttle
stay

Adjectives

satisfied
complimentary

Sam Monroe checked out of the hotel.

Alberto asked Sam to fill out a comment card.

Sam checked the boxes on the questionnaire and wrote a comment at the end.

He dropped the card in a box.

Sam asked about the complimentary airport shuttle.

The next shuttle would leave in 5 minutes.

Sam waited in the lobby...

...until the shuttle arrived.

Culture and Language

- A *comment* is a short statement.
- When you *check* a box, you mark in the box of your choice.

- *Complimentary* means "at no charge; free."

Personal Hygiene, Health, and Grooming in the Hospitality Business

The image of a hotel depends on the people who work there. Hospitality workers must present themselves as clean, healthy, and well-groomed. Here are 20 basic steps toward this goal.

1. Brush your teeth.

2. Shower every day before going to work.

3. Men should shave every day. Most hotels do not allow beards. If the hotel allows moustaches, they should be kept neatly trimmed.

4. Use underarm deodorant.

5. Keep your hair neatly cut.

6. Do not use extreme (bright red or yellow, green, etc.) hair coloring.

7. Do not overuse hair gel, mousse, or hairspray.

8. Men should keep their hair somewhat short. It should not touch their shirt collars.

9. Women with long hair should tie it back in a ponytail or pin it up and back.

10. Do not overuse make-up. Lipstick should not be too bright or very dark.

11. Do not wear perfume or cologne. Some guests are allergic to these scents.

12. Wash your hands frequently.

13. Keep your fingernails neatly trimmed. Long fingernails may harbor germs that cause diseases.

14. If you must blow your nose or sneeze, use a handkerchief. Never put your finger in your nose or mouth.

15. Do not come to work if you are sick. This is especially important for restaurant workers.

16. Keep your uniform clean and well pressed.

17. Do not wear long earrings, long necklaces, or other jewelry that could easily get caught on things.

18. Never smoke in or around the hotel.

19. Never drink alcohol before going to work or while you are on duty.

20. Get enough sleep, exercise regularly, and eat healthy foods.

Effective Practices for Hospitality Professionals

> For each hospitality job mentioned in this book, certain practices can bring efficiency and a high level of customer satisfaction. Here are some crucial practices for each of the key jobs below.

Bartender

- Serve bar customers pleasantly and without inviting conflict.
- Give priority to orders that servers bring in from the tables.
- Make drinks neither too strong nor too weak.

Bell Person

- Be knowledgeable about the operation of all systems in the room (lights, heating/cooling, the safe, etc.).
- Do not obviously wait for a tip. Once you have finished settling a guest into a room, exit the room promptly.
- Treat luggage carefully and respectfully.
- Bring baggage promptly to a room. The guest should not have to wait more than 5 minutes for you to arrive.

Concierge

- Stay knowledgeable about local attractions and services by reading local newspapers, checking relevant Websites, and maintaining connections with service providers (taxi cab companies, doctors' offices, etc.)
- Follow up promptly on any promises made to guests. If you said you would check on something, check on it now and get back to the guest within 10 minutes.
- Project confidence, knowledge, and a willingness to serve.

Driver

- Above all, project an image of confidence and a commitment to safety.
- When in radio contact with the hotel or other drivers, remember that the guests can hear you. Keep your radio contact short and businesslike.
- Treat every piece of luggage gently, as if it contained breakable items.
- Stay informed about local construction projects or other things that might create traffic jams. Seek alternate routes to avoid long waits on the road.

Event Planner

- Do not give any information that you are unsure about. Customers will be offended if you promise something and later you have to retract your promise.
- Sell the hotel's services, but do not sound like a sales person. Suggest possibilities instead of pushing the product.
- Follow up frequently with potential customers.

Front Desk Clerk

- Confirm all details about the room assignment (smoking/non-smoking, size of bed, etc.)
- Confirm each room rate and room number by showing the guest on paper, not by speaking such details out loud so others can hear.
- Make sure payment details are worked out (credit card/check/cash, etc.)
- Make the guest feel welcome. Use his or her name at least once in the check-in and check-out processes.

Front Desk Manager

- Settle disputes about room assignments, reservations, etc. pleasantly and without confrontation.
- Support the desk clerks in carrying out hotel policies.
- Compensate—with free upgrades, rate reductions, meal vouchers, or other benefits—guests who feel wronged.

Housekeeper

- Respect the guest's privacy.
- Do not throw away or re-arrange papers or other business-related items in the guest's room.
- Be generous with amenities like soap, shampoo, or coffee-making materials.

Parking Valet

- Drive slowly and cautiously. Treat every guest's car with the utmost care.
- Never eat, drink, or smoke in a guest's car.
- If you adjust seats or mirrors or radio stations, return them to the original settings before you leave the car.
- When taking a car out of the garage for a guest, do so as soon as the guest requests the car. Guests should not be kept waiting more than 5 minutes.

Restaurant Server

- Bring drinks, bread and butter, etc. soon after customers are seated.
- Establish rapport with customers by giving solid answers and advice about the menu.
- Check back often to make sure the customer is satisfied.
- Be friendly but not intrusive. The customer looks to you for service, not for chatter.

Restaurant Host / Hostess

- Welcome every customer sincerely and pleasantly.
- Seat guests as quickly as possible.
- Settle any disputes between wait staff and customers by making the customer feel special and appreciated.

Room Service Specialist

- Always repeat an order to confirm it. Mistakes annoy the guest and cost the hotel money.
- Try to sell the hotel's services, but do not sound like a sales person. Make suggestions instead of pushing the product: "May I suggest...?" "Perhaps you'd like to consider...."
- Give the guest an accurate estimate of time until delivery of the food. The guest will be annoyed if food remains undelivered after the time you estimated.
- Be flexible. If the guest requests something that is not on the menu, check to see if the kitchen can provide it anyway. Then promptly get back to the guest.

Common Items in the Hospitality Business: A Visual Glossary

adapter

ambulance

armchair

back seat

bag

baggage claim

bar

bathroom

bathtub

bedsheet

black pepper

bottle

boxed lunch

briefcase

buffet

bus schedule

business card

button

car door

car keys

card reader

carpet

cart

cash register

cashier

check

chef

clipboard

closet

clothes

 coach

coffee table

 coffeemaker

combination lock

cork

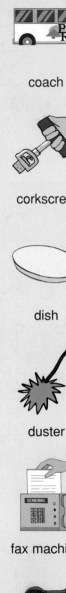 corkscrew

cover

 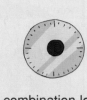 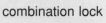 credit card

desk

dessert

dish

 double room

drapes

drawer

driver's seat

duster

elevator

emergency room

executive lounge

exercise bike

fax machine

 fork

  front desk

glass

 guest laundry

hairdryer

headlights

 hostess station

 hot tub

 key card

  king bed

   kitchen

 knife

  label

 laundry bag

leak	lobby	lobster	luggage	luggage stand
luggage tag	luggage trolley	mailbox	map	menu
minibar	mirror	museum	note	omelet
outlet	parcel	parking garage	passport	pen
pillow	plate	plug	pocket	postcard
queen bed	questionnaire	rear-view mirror	registration form	remote control
revolving door	roll-away bed	safe	screen	seat belt

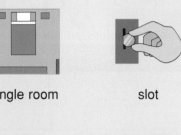 seating chart

 shampoo

 shower stall

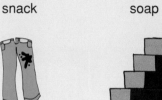 shuttle

 silverware

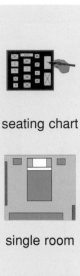 single room

 slot

 snack

 soap

 sofa bed

 sponge

 spoon

 stain

 stairs

 stair-stepper

 steak

 suitcase

 swimming pool

 swimsuit

 tablet

 taxi

 telephone

 television

 thermostat

 ticket

 toilet

 toiletries

 toothbrush

 towel

 traveler's checks

 tray

 treadmill

 trunk

 twin bed

 umbrella

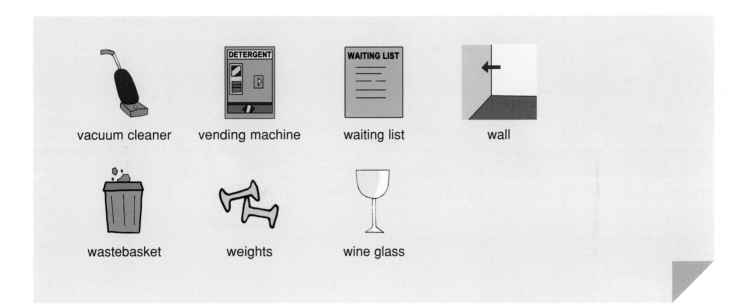

vacuum cleaner   vending machine   waiting list   wall

wastebasket   weights   wine glass